Thanksgiving

Samantha Bell

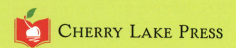

Published in the United States of America by Cherry Lake Publishing Group
Ann Arbor, Michigan
www.cherrylakepublishing.com

Reading Adviser: Beth Walker Gambro, MS, Ed., Reading Consultant, Yorkville, IL
Content Adviser: Heather Bruegl, M.A. (Oneida/Stockbridge-Munsee) Historian-Indigenous Consultant-Lecturer

Photo Credits: cover, page 28: © MyTravelCurator/Shutterstock; page 5: cover of *The Mayflower Pilgrims* by Edmund J. Carpenter, Abingdon Press, gift of Claremont School of Theology, Internet Archive; page 6: Detroit Publishing Company, Library of Congress; pages 7, 15, 20, 22, 23: Library of Congress; page 8: © Everett Collection/Shutterstock; page 11: © David Persson/Shutterstock; page 12: Georg Braun; Frans Hogenberg: Cities of the World, Band 1, 1572, Heidelberg University via Wikimedia Commons; page 16: © Plymouth 400, Inc.; page 19: © Gordon Swanson/Shutterstock; page 25: © Michael Gordon/Shutterstock; pages 26, 29: © Associated Press; page 27: © Billy Wilson/Flickr (CC BY-NC 2.0)

Cherry Lake Press is an imprint of Cherry Lake Publishing Group.

Library of Congress Cataloging-in-Publication Data has been filed and is available at catalog.loc.gov.

Cherry Lake Publishing Group would like to acknowledge the work of the Partnership for 21st Century Learning, a Network of Battelle for Kids. Please visit http://www.battelleforkids.org/networks/p21 for more information.

Printed in the United States of America
Corporate Graphics

Note from publisher: Websites change regularly, and their future contents are outside of our control. Supervise children when conducting any recommended online searches for extended learning opportunities.

Samantha Bell was born and raised near Orlando, Florida. She grew up in a family of eight kids and all kinds of pets, including goats, chickens, cats, dogs, rabbits, horses, parakeets, hamsters, guinea pigs, a monkey, a raccoon, and a coatimundi. She now lives with her family in the foothills of the Blue Ridge Mountains, where she enjoys hiking, painting, and snuggling with their cats Pocket, Pebble, and Mr. Tree-Tree Triggers.

CONTENTS

CHAPTER 1

The Story People Tell

A Celebration of Survival

In the early 1600s, the law in England stated that everyone had to belong to the Church of England. But a group of people believed that the church's teachings were wrong. They thought the church was not following the teachings of the Bible. They wanted to worship God in their own way. They decided they had to separate from the church. For this reason, they were called Separatists.

But the Church of England was in control. People who disagreed with the church were punished. The Separatists began holding their religious services secretly. It was the only way to avoid arrest and **persecution**. In 1608, some Separatists escaped to the Netherlands.

The Separatists were Puritans. They followed strict rules.

But life in the Netherlands was not easy. In 1620, some of the Separatists decided to start again in the New World. They called themselves Pilgrims.

In July, they boarded two ships, the *Speedwell* and the *Mayflower*. But soon after they left, the *Speedwell* started taking on water. Those who wanted to continue the trip boarded the *Mayflower*. The ship was crowded with 102 passengers and 30 crew members.

The Pilgrims planned to create a new settlement in Virginia. But during the journey, storms blew the ship too far north. They landed on Cape Cod in November. They finally chose a site for their settlement on December 21. By the time winter set in, they had only a few homes completed. Many of the Pilgrims continued to live on board the *Mayflower*. They did not have enough food for the winter. More than half died from hunger and sickness.

Passengers signed The Mayflower Compact. It set rules and laws for the colony.

When spring came, the remaining Pilgrims had to learn how to farm in the New World. This is the story people still tell today. It is a story of friendship and celebration. The story says that a Native American man named Squanto came to help them. Squanto spoke English.

Images such as this present a fictional story of the relationship between the two groups.

He shared seeds with the Pilgrims. They planted corn, pumpkins, and beans. Squanto taught them how to place dead fish beneath the seeds. The fish **fertilized** the seeds and helped the crops grow.

In the fall, the crops were ready to **harvest**. There was plenty to eat. The Pilgrims decided to have a big feast.

The story says that the Pilgrims wanted to show thanks to the Native Americans. It says they invited the Native Americans to the feast. The Pilgrims served them corn, pumpkins, turkey, and bread. They thanked God for a good harvest. The feast became known as the first Thanksgiving. People use this story to teach about helping others. They use it to teach gratitude. This story makes people feel good. Too bad it didn't happen like that.

The *real* story is not that simple. But it is much more interesting.

LIFE IN THE NETHERLANDS

The Separatists found religious freedom in the Netherlands. But they struggled in their new homeland. In England, they were farmers, raising their own food. In the Netherlands, they had to work in the **textile mills**. They had to learn a new language and new customs. They were also worried about their children. They wanted their children to grow up English. But their children were becoming part of Dutch society.

In 1620, some Separatists decided to start again in the New World. They would be able to worship freely and keep their English culture. They would be able to farm again.

CHAPTER 2

The Facts of the Matter

A Tense Truce

The story often told about the first Thanksgiving leaves out key facts. These details are important for understanding history and the way it shaped our world today. The story many have heard begins with British citizens setting a course for religious freedom. The *history* begins with a kidnapping.

Tisquantum was a member of the Patuxet, a coastal band of the Wampanoag. He was born around 1580. In 1614, Thomas Hunt, an English captain, kidnapped Tisquantum and 23 other Nauset and Patuxet people. The Nauset were another Wampanoag band. Captain John Smith had left Hunt in charge. Smith wanted Hunt to trade with the local people. Instead, Hunt captured them. Smith and others were angry at Hunt's betrayal.

The Wampanoag people had lived in the area for around 12,000 years before European arrival.

Records show that Hunt sailed to the port of Málaga in Spain. This illustration of Málaga was created in 1572.

Hunt sailed to Spain. He sold the kidnapped people into slavery. Spanish **monks** rescued some of the people before Hunt sold them. Tisquantum was one of the rescued. The monks wanted to spread their Christian faith. They taught it to the people they freed. Tisquantum found a way from Spain to England where he learned to speak English. He got a job as an interpreter and returned to North America. His job was to help set up fur trade.

Trading had not been going well for Europeans in New England. After Tisquantum and the others' kidnapping, the Nauset and Patuxet people got angry. They refused to trade. They drove the Europeans away. They burned at least one ship. But the Europeans had carried diseases.

JOINING THE COLONY

© Christine Hochkeppel – USA TODAY NETWORK

Tisquantum became an important member of the Plymouth colony. He served as an emissary between the Wampanoag and the Pilgrims. He helped make trade agreements. He also understood how distrustful both sides were. He used that distrust for his own gain. He spread lies. He tried to convince the Pilgrims that Ousamequin was planning to attack. He told the Wampanoag and other groups that the Pilgrims stored diseases in barrels. Tisquantum threatened to release the barrels if people didn't do what he wanted. The Pilgrims and the Wampanoag discovered his lies. Ousamequin wanted the Pilgrims to hand Tisquantum over for justice. The Pilgrims depended on Tisquantum. They did not hand him over. Tisquantum was shunned by the Wampanoag for treason. Still, in 1622, Tisquantum got sick on a trading journey with the Plymouth governor. He died a few days later. Some think his death was suspicious. They think he may have been poisoned.

The Patuxet and other Indigenous peoples did not have any **immunity** to European diseases. By the time Tisquantum returned in 1619, the Patuxet people were dead. Their towns were destroyed. A "Great Dying" had swept across the land for 3 years. Tisquantum's home and people were gone. He went to live with other Wampanoag people. The Wampanoag leader, Ousamequin, did not trust him. He held Tisquantum as a captive.

In the spring of 1621, a man named Samoset visited Ousamequin. Samoset was an Abenaki leader from what is now Maine. He had learned some English words from the fishermen there. Ousamequin told Samoset that a group of Europeans had settled nearby. He asked Samoset to go investigate. Ousamequin and the other Wampanoag were suspicious.

Samoset went and spoke with the European group. It was the group of only 50 Separatists who had survived the winter. Samoset's greeting surprised them. "Welcome, Englishmen," he told them. The Pilgrims needed help. They had women and children with them. They were starving. Samoset told them about the Patuxet who had died. He told them that Massasoit was the leader in the area. Massasoit was Ousamequin's title. The Pilgrims thought it was his name.

This 19th century engraving shows Ousamequin meeting with Governor Carver. It was created nearly 300 years after the event shown.

Throughout 1621, the Pilgrims complained when friendly Wampanoag people came to visit. They were worried about sharing their food. They asked Ousamequin to keep his people away. Here, a historic interpreter demonstrates traditional Wampanoag cooking.

Samoset returned to the Wampanoag to tell them what he had learned. Ousamequin agreed to meet the Pilgrims. He brought Tisquantum as an interpreter. The Pilgrims called Tisquantum Squanto. Tisquantum helped them make a **treaty** with Ousamequin and the Wampanoag. Both groups promised to protect each other from attacks, among other things. Tisquantum also showed them how to fish, plant corn, and gather berries and nuts. Like in the story, Tisquantum taught the Pilgrims to bury dead fish under the seeds to help them grow. And the crops did grow.

The growing season passed and harvest time began. The Wampanoag heard gunshots from near the Plymouth colony. They were not usual hunting sounds. Ousamequin gathered 90 Wampanoag warriors. They may have thought the Pilgrims were being attacked or were starting a war.

The Pilgrims were not under attack or starting a war. They were celebrating. They had decided to hold a feast. They had grown enough food for the winter. They would not starve. Four men had gone out to shoot wild birds. They shot so many in one day that it was enough to last a whole week. They also began firing their guns in the air over and over again to celebrate.

Ousamequin arrived with his men, surprising the Pilgrims. The Pilgrims offered to share their food, but there was not enough for so many. Ousamequin sent his men into the woods to hunt. They killed five deer to add to the feast. The Wampanoag stayed for 3 days.

CHAPTER 3

Spinning the Story

A Campaign for Gratitude

The Pilgrims' feast was not the first Thanksgiving. It was just a feast to celebrate a good harvest. For the Pilgrims, a thanksgiving was actually a time of prayer and **fasting**. The idea of a feast of thanksgiving would come much later.

Over the years, the colonies held many days of thanksgiving and fasting. When the United States became a country, it continued to set aside days of thanksgiving. For example, in 1789, President George Washington called for a day of thanks. He wanted the country to celebrate the end of the American Revolution (1775–1783) and the adoption of the new Constitution. Later presidents issued similar **proclamations**. These included John Adams and James Madison. Still, there was no yearly Thanksgiving celebration for the whole nation.

The origins of Thanksgiving have little to do with Indigenous people, who were never consulted or included. Still, even today, celebrations of the holiday center on traditional Indigenous foods such as corn, pumpkin, squash, and beans.

Sarah Josepha Hale's ideas about giving thanks were separate from the story we know today.

In 1827, writer Sarah Josepha Hale published a novel. She had grown up in New England. People there had a day of thanks every year. In her book, she wrote about the tradition. By 1837, Hale was the editor of a magazine for women called *Godey's Lady's Book*. She began to write essays about giving thanks. She believed the whole country should celebrate an **annual** day of thanksgiving together. At the time, the states were becoming more and more divided. Tensions over **states' rights** to enslave people were growing between the Northern and Southern states. Conflicts over western expansion were rising, too. Hale thought a holiday like Thanksgiving might help bring the nation back together.

It was during this difficult time that the idea of the first Thanksgiving was established. In 1841, a pastor named Alexander Young published a book called *Chronicles of the Pilgrim Fathers*. In the book, he printed a letter by Edward Winslow. Winslow was a Pilgrim at the feast in 1621. He was also a Pilgrim representative who visited local Indigenous leaders with Tisquantum. The letter talks about the 3-day harvest celebration.

Young added some lines of his own. He described the event as "the first Thanksgiving, the harvest festival of New England." He also said that the Pilgrims probably ate wild turkey as well as deer. Alexander had mixed up the harvest festival with days of giving thanks and fasting. But the idea stuck. Because of those few lines, people believed the Pilgrims' feast with the Native Americans was the first Thanksgiving.

Thanksgiving was not yet a national holiday. But Sarah Hale had not given up. In 1846, she started a letter-writing campaign. Every year, she wrote two articles about why the country needed a national Thanksgiving holiday. She asked her readers to encourage public officials to establish the holiday. She wrote thousands of letters to elected officials. She wrote to other magazine editors. She also wrote to well-known preachers. By 1854, more than 30 states and U.S. territories had established their own Thanksgiving celebrations.

PICK A THURSDAY

For many years, the president could choose what day Thanksgiving would be celebrated. President Lincoln chose the last Thursday in November. Every other president did the same until 1939. That year, President Franklin Roosevelt was dealing with the Great Depression (1929–1939). He decided to move Thanksgiving up a week. That would make the Christmas shopping season longer. He thought it might help the economy. But 16 states refused to change the date. Two Thanksgiving holidays were celebrated. In 1941, Roosevelt gave in. Congress passed a resolution returning the date to the fourth Thursday.

Abraham Lincoln's son, Todd, grew attached to a turkey intended for Thanksgiving. President Lincoln told White House staff to save it.

Hale went even further. In 1863, she wrote to President Abraham Lincoln. By this time, the country had suffered a great deal. The North and South had been fighting the Civil War (1861–1865) for 2 years. Thousands of men on both sides had died. Lincoln agreed with Hale that a day of thanksgiving might help. He issued a proclamation in October. He stated that the fourth Thursday of November would be a National Day of Thanksgiving. In 1870, Congress passed legislation making Thanksgiving a national holiday.

CHAPTER 4

Writing History

Gathering Sources

People today know what happened in 1621 because of primary sources. Primary sources are written by people who experienced an event. The writings of two Pilgrim leaders, William Bradford and Edward Winslow, provide detailed records. William Bradford became the first governor of Plymouth Colony. He wrote about the Pilgrims' experiences in a journal called *Of Plymouth Plantation*. It provides a firsthand account of their everyday lives. Bradford's journal became the authoritative record of Plymouth Colony.

WILLIAM BRADFORD
GOVERNOR and HISTORIAN
OF THE
PLYMOUTH COLONY

BORN IN AUSTERFIELD, ENGLAND-1590
DIED IN PLYMOUTH, NEW ENGLAND-1657

William Bradford's journal is a primary source. But it only shows one perspective.

This display showcases living relatives of the Pilgrims and the Wampanoag of 1620 for the 400th anniversary of the Plymouth Colony.

In his journal, Bradford talks about how the Pilgrims prepared for the second winter. He mentions gathering the harvest. Those who were skilled fishermen provided fish for every family. Others killed wild turkeys and deer for meat. They had so much food that year that some even wrote about it to their friends in England.

More of the story was described by Edward Winslow. Winslow was responsible for communication between colonists and the Wampanoag people. Winslow writes about many of these experiences. In the letter that Alexander Young published, Winslow included details about the actual feast. He described how they fired their guns in celebration. He talked about Chief Massasoit (Ousamequin) and the 90 men who came with him. He also mentioned different types of food they enjoyed.

Using these accounts, historians are able to piece together most of what happened that day. One more letter by William Hilton helps fill in the gaps. Hilton was a passenger on the ship called the *Fortune*. It arrived at Plymouth right after the feast in 1621. In the letter, Hilton discussed other foods that were available when he arrived.

A DIFFERENT POINT OF VIEW

Not everyone in the United States celebrates the Thanksgiving holiday. For many Indigenous peoples, it represents a time of loss. Instead of Thanksgiving, they recognize a National Day of Mourning. Ninety percent of Native people living in Massachusetts died in 1616 from unknown diseases. In all of New England, where once 140,000 Indigenous peoples may have lived, only 10,000 remained by 1675.

The people of the Plymouth Colony demanded many things from the Wampanoag. They gave little in return. Fifty years later, a great war took place between the settlers and the Wampanoags, as well as other Native nations. It became known as King Phillip's War (1675–1676). There was much bloodshed. In the end, the Native nations were not able to drive the settlers out of New England.

Mercy given to starving people led to centuries of loss. Still, the Wampanoag and their traditions endured.

Today, books, articles, museums, and living history presentations help tell the true story of the past. The Wampanoag, along with other Indigenous and non-Indigenous groups, work to end the fictions.

Activity
Finding the Time

This book mentions many dates. Create a timeline that includes at least 10 of these dates. Then choose at least 10 other important dates in American history to add to your timeline.

Dates from the book:

1580 – Tisquantum is born.

1608 – The Pilgrims arrive in the Netherlands.

1614 – Tisquantum is kidnapped.

1619 – Tisquantum returns, but his people are gone.

1620 – The Pilgrims arrive at Plymouth.

1621 – The first Thanksgiving takes place.

1789 – President George Washington calls for a National Day of Thanks.

1827 – Sarah Josepha Hale publishes a novel, which includes a day of thanks.

1837 – Hale becomes editor of *Godey's Lady's Book* magazine and writes articles about Thanksgiving.

1841 – Alexander Young publishes a letter describing the Pilgrims' feast.

1846 – Hale begins her letter-writing campaign.

1863 – Hale writes to President Lincoln requesting a national holiday.

1870 – Congress makes Thanksgiving a national holiday.

1939 – President Roosevelt moves Thanksgiving from the second to the third Thursday in November.

1941 – Congress sets Thanksgiving on the last Thursday of November.

Learn More

Books

Byers, Ann. *Squanto.* New York, NY: Cavendish Square, 2021.

Holub, Joan. *What Was the First Thanksgiving?* New York, NY: Penguin Workshop, 2013.

Isabell, Hannah. *Squanto: Native American Translator and Guide.* New York, NY: Enslow Publishing, 2018.

McDonnell, Julia. *The Pilgrims Didn't Celebrate the First Thanksgiving.* New York, NY: Gareth Stevens Publishing, 2017.

On the Web

With an adult, learn more online with these suggested searches.

"Thanksgiving in North America: American Indian Perspectives," Smithsonian

"Thanksgiving in North America: Where Did Your Favorite Thanksgiving Food Originate?" Smithsonian

"The First Thanksgiving," National Geographic Kids

"You Are the Historian Game," Plimoth Patuxet Museums

Glossary

annual (AHN-yoo-uhl) something that happens once every year

fasting (FAST-ing) a time of eating no food

fertilized (FUHR-tuh-lyzd) added substances to plants to make them stronger and able to produce more

harvest (HAR-vuhst) the season or process of gathering in ripe crops

immunity (im-YOO-nuh-tee) a body's protection from sickness

monks (MUHNKS) men who have joined other men in a religious community and vowed to live a simple life

persecution (puhr-sih-KYOO-shuhn) the act of continually treating someone cruelly because of their race, religion, or some other difference

proclamations (prah-kluh-MAY-shuhns) official announcements

states' rights (STAYTS RYTS) the rights and powers held by individual states rather than the federal government

textile mills (TEK-styl MIHLZ) factories that produce cloth from yarn or other fibers

treaty (TREE-tee) an agreement between different groups made by negotiation

Index